For Bix.

Published by The Baben

All rights reserved.
No portion of this book may be reproduced in any form without permission from the publisher, except as permitted by U.S. copyright law.

Copyright © 2023 The Baben

This book is a work of fiction. Names, characters, events, and incidents are the products of the author's imagination. Any resemblance to actual persons, living or dead, or actual events is purely coincidental.

www.booksbythebaben.com

Printed in the USA

1 3 6 10 15 21 28 36

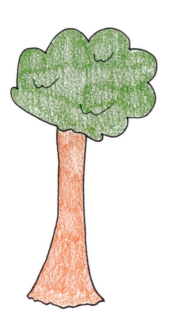

This garbage truck is blue.

This garbage truck is green.

This garbage truck has 3 blue circles on it.

This garbage truck has 2 red squares on it.

This garbage truck is driving fast.

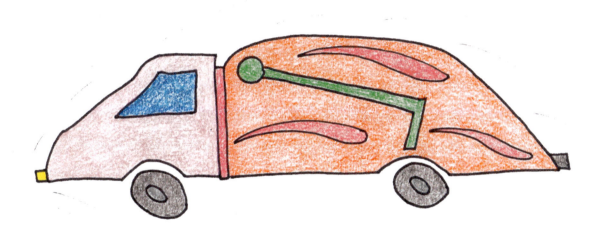

This garbage truck is driving slow.

This garbage truck is big.

This garbage truck is small.

This garbage truck lives on a farm.

This garbage truck lives in the city.

This garbage truck is upside down!

Now it's right side up!

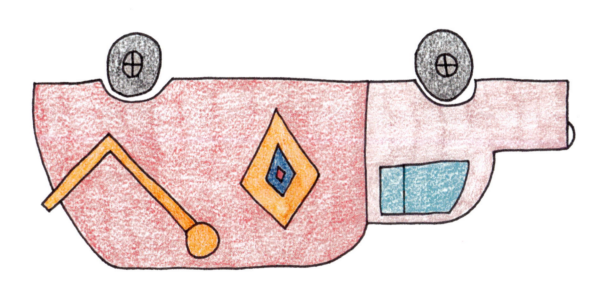

This garbage truck doesn't have any wheels.

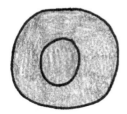 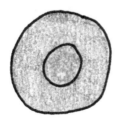

This garbage truck is sad.

This garbage truck is happy.

Now all the garbage trucks are sleepy.

Goodnight garbage trucks.

If you like this book please support us with an Amazon review!

Visit www.booksbythebaben.com to join our mailing list and be the first to hear about new titles.

Adulting (inspired by stuff grown-ups do)

 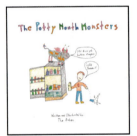

Get a plant, they said.
It'll be fun, they said.

Meet Gobb Pucking Bammit, Pizza Bucking Bit, Howlee Sitt, and other silly potty mouth monsters in this soon-to-be-award-winning children's book.

Things That Go (no explanation needed)

The title says it all.
If your kid loves trains then they will love this book.

The title says it all.
If your kid loves garbage trucks then they will love this book.

Pen Fifteen Club (innocent stories full of innuendo)

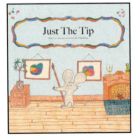 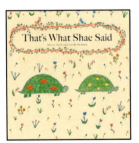 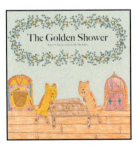

Henry has a paintbrush, but no paint. Cindy has paint, but no paintbrush. When they discover their complementary interests Henry and Cindy work together to make their dreams come true.

The journey will be long and hard. That's what Shae said! Join Shelly and Chester as they follow advice from the wise owl Shae and search for a new pond to call home.

Relax, they're just chipmunks, and it's a golden shower of *wheat*. Get your mind out of the gutter.

Made in the USA
Las Vegas, NV
25 January 2024